IN THE STUDIO WITH
JUDY MURRAH

Linda Lewis

IN THE STUDIO WITH
JUDY MURRAH

12 PLAYFUL QUILTED PROJECTS

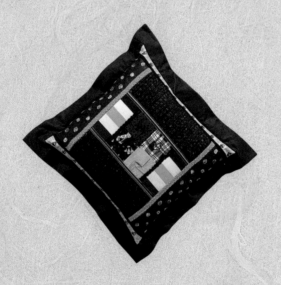

JUDY MURRAH

Martingale™
& COMPANY

In the Studio with Judy Murrah: 12 Playful Quilted Projects
© 2001 by Judy Murrah

Martingale ™
& C O M P A N Y

That Patchwork Place®

That Patchwork Place® is an imprint of
Martingale & Company™

Martingale & Company
20205 144th Avenue NE
Woodinville, WA 98072-8478
www.martingale-pub.com

Printed in the USA
06 05 04 03 02 01   8 7 6 5 4 3 2 1

Library of Congress Cataloging-in-Publication Data

Murrah, Judy
   In the studio with Judy Murrah : 12 playful quilted
projects / by Judy Murrah.
         p.   cm.
      ISBN 1-56477-300-0
         1. Patchwork—Patterns.   2. Quilted goods.   I. Title.

TT535.M85 2001
746.46'041—dc21
                                     00–065356

Mission Statement

We are dedicated to providing quality products and service by working together to inspire creativity and to enrich the lives we touch.

Credits

President . . . . Nancy J. Martin
CEO . . . . Daniel J. Martin
Publisher . . . . Jane Hamada
Editorial Director . . . . Mary V. Green
Editorial Project Manger . . . . Tina Cook
Technical Editor . . . . Barbara Weiland
Copy Editor . . . . Karen Koll
Design and Production Manager . . . . Stan Green
Illustrator . . . . Laurel Strand
Cover and Text Designer . . . . Trina Stahl
Location Photographer . . . . Pat Mercer
Project Photographer . . . . Brent Kane

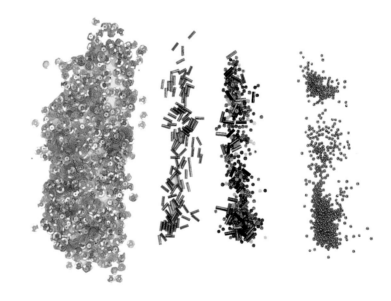

Dedication

To Grammy's little Snickerdoodle, Madison Elizabeth Murrah,
who likes to "decorate" quilts.

Acknowledgments

I am grateful to have my brilliant editor, Barbara Weiland, back on my team again.
Her constant encouragement and guidance were invaluable
during the writing of each of my books.

Praises to my mom. Her gentleness will be with me always.

And love and thanks to my Quilts, Inc. buddies, Karey, Willie, Nancy H.,
and Nancy O. for their friendship. "We will always have Paris."

And to Kim DeCoste, whose constant help and support I could not do without.

And to Beatrice Steffek, who faithfully comes to my sewing rescue.

And, last but not least, I say thank you to the manufacturers
whose materials I love and use. Special thanks to:
Bernina of America
Omnigrid
The Warm Company
Sulky of America
Fasco Fabric Sales
Fairfield Processing

Contents

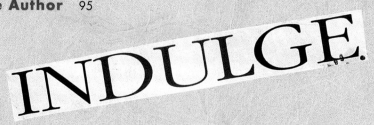

INDULGE

Introduction:
Welcome to My Playroom!

▶▶▶ WHILE YOU MAY not think of a sewing studio as a playroom, I do! Working with fabric and color is like child's play for me! I started sewing and creating when I was a little girl, and sewing has continued to be the greatest creative passion of my adult life. I have not always had an ideal work space for my sewing, though. I have worked on a discarded coffee table in a room I shared with my two older sisters, in a corner of a utility room, and in a walk-in closet. I've sewn in a study and in the sitting area of our master bedroom.

If you're anything like me, you've done (or are still doing) the same. Last year, one of my lifelong dreams came true—a real studio just for me. After working for years in whatever space I could carve out in our home for designing and sewing, I feel like the luckiest quilter alive!

Visualization, organization, meditation, and relaxation are all important ingredients in my design and sewing process. I need them all to be happy and productive, and my husband and I considered them all, plus other elements, as we transformed our 25' x 26' garage into my quilt and color playroom. I wish all of you the good fortune of somewhere wonderful to dream, design, and work.

Let There Be Light!

THE FIRST THING on my list was lots of windows for lots of light! Light has been important to me for as long as I can remember—or at least as far back as the fifth grade. Our teacher kept the shades drawn every afternoon most of the year—without sunshine, every school day was pretty depressing for me.

Unlike that schoolroom, my new studio is stimulating and inviting, with five sets of twin windows measuring 36" x 60" each. Often I look up from my sewing into my beautiful yard for renewed energy and brief relaxation. And I can leave the studio through the back door to walk outside when I need a little fresh air. Even in the Texas heat, a little break taken out in the garden is refreshing and revitalizing.

A Place for Everything and Everything in Its Place!

ORGANIZATION WAS NEXT on my list. In order to have the freedom to play at my quiltmaking when the next great idea strikes, I collect buttons, beads, lace (both old and new), threads, trims, charms, trinkets, ribbons of all kinds, gadgets, tools, rulers, and fabric. It's important for me to be able to see all these things or to know where I can find them quickly and easily. For the most efficient use of my time and space, it's important to me to be able to put everything back in place when a project is completed. However, while a work is in progress, my studio may appear to be in complete chaos as I surround myself with lots of choices and stimuli. What may look chaotic does have a sense of order to me, but before I start a new project, I put everything back in place so I can start with a clean "canvas."

> **CUTTING IN COMFORT**
My cutting mat rests on a counter-height table on wheels. It's a great place to work when I'm planning a quilt.

Doing the Improv

MY DEAR MOM instilled in me two slogans that still govern much of my work:

"Use it up, wear it out. Make it do or do without."

"Waste not, want not."

Most of my current designs are spontaneous and start with scraps—some big, some small. I rarely begin with a set plan, and I encourage you to do the same, using the directions in this book as a springboard. Don't try to copy them—do something different to make the work your own. Even if not everything you do is totally successful, giving yourself the permission to play and to learn from what does work—as well as what doesn't—is one of the best ways to grow as a designer.

I love using the stuff I already have on hand to do improvisational quiltmaking. I take great pleasure in using pieces and patchwork left over from another project or something someone else started and then decided not to finish. Castoffs and sale items from craft stores, dime stores, quilt shops, thrift stores, and antique or junk stores are my best working treasures. Many evenings I find myself working well into the night after finding an exciting new treasure to incorporate into a current project or to use as a starter for the next one!

Up on the Wall

A PLACE TO design and constant visual pleasure and excitement keep me going through the design and sewing process. My 8' x 14½' design wall, constructed of Celotex covered with Warm and Natural cotton batting, provides plenty of space for arranging and viewing finished sections of a quilt or garment so that I can evaluate my work and decide on changes or additions. I pin fabrics and embellishments to one end of the design wall to audition them for the project as I'm working.

Jump-Start Me with Color

COLOR! SURROUND ME with color. There is not a color I don't like or would not use. Of course, the bolder and brighter it is, the better to my eyes. If you always work in pastels or particular color combinations, I challenge you to spread your wings and try

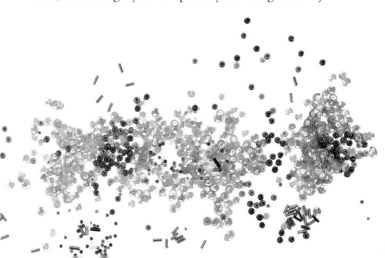

► TREASURE, NOT TRASH

Keep a tin or open box near your cutting mat. As you cut pieces for a project, put the fabric leftovers in the container. When it's full, transfer the snippets to a larger container; a plastic storage box for shoes works well. When you're ready to piece a Crazy quilt or need strips for stitch-and-flip additions to blocks, you'll have a variety of scraps just waiting to be used.

something else as you experiment with the designs and techniques presented in this book.

Most often I work on something to please myself, but I do love an appreciative audience, and I strive to create something that will appeal to the viewer as well. My goal with any piece is to draw the viewer into my work to study and maybe even to meditate over it. Much of it is symbolic of old and new expe-

riences of joy and pain, happiness and sadness. I also love to make quilts to celebrate and document life's big and little events. Although the viewer may not know what the symbols mean to me, they can often see something from their own experiences in my work, make up their own story about what it means, or enjoy it for what it is—a work of joy and colorful creativity.

Add Some Inspiration

KEY TO ALL of my creativity is the importance of being in the right state of mind. Music I love and the glow of a scented candle are indispensable for setting my mind at ease and giving it room to come up with innovative ideas. When you visit my playroom, you'll often hear Andrea Bocelli, strains of Bach, or the soundtrack from *Ever After* playing in the background. I encourage you to surround yourself with things you love and to add the richness of personal ritual to your workspace. It makes a difference!

► EASY PICKUP

Use a rough-sided scrubbing pad from the household department in your grocery store to brush away lint, small slivers of fabric, and batting from your work surface, ironing board, and cutting mat before you start your next project.

Snips and Snippets

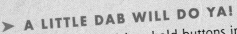

> ## ➤ A LITTLE DAB WILL DO YA!

Use a dab of gluestick to hold buttons in place while you hand or machine stitch them to your quilt or garment.

> ## ➤ EMBELLISHING ON THE GO

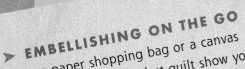

Place a paper shopping bag or a canvas tote (perhaps from the last quilt show you attended) in your sewing area, and tuck 5 to 10 snack-size, self-sealing plastic bags inside. Fill the bags with bits of leftover trim and lace plus extra buttons, Yo-Yos, Prairie Points, and beads. (I use the plastic bags to sort like items together.) When you're on your way somewhere, grab the shopping bag and a project that needs embellishing. It's fun to see how you can use these little tidbits. "Waste not, want not" is my motto!

> ## ➤ NOT OUT OF SORTS

Long ago I got smart and sorted my old pearl buttons, rhinestone buttons, and 1930s buttons into separate containers, but I always had to rummage through the rest of my button collection to find just what I needed for a project. Now I simply grab the appropriate photo file box. These are relatively inexpensive and are available covered in pretty papers. Keep your eye out for them on sale at craft, discount, drug, and grocery stores. You can slip an identifying card into a metal holder at one end of the box. I sort my buttons by color and label my boxes that way. Divide the box interior with strips of heavy cardboard so you can sort by color family or button type in each box.

MAKE A WISH

► DINING IN

My studio is so pleasant that my husband and I often eat our evening meal at the library table. We enjoy the view and the brightly colored atmosphere of the room. The work on the design wall is always an evolving piece of fabric art.

you fill my heart with happiness

► IRONING TABLE

My ironing table gives me lots of room for working on large projects. I had a solid-core door cut to fit on my antique library table and wrapped it in Warm and Natural batting. The batting is covered with Teflon-coated ironing-board fabric. Wood strips mounted to the bottom raise it from the surface of the table to a comfortable working height. The ironing table provides an open space where I can store an extra cutting mat, a roll of pattern paper, and small trays for pins, scissors, pencils, papers, and other small tools. I love having everything at my fingertips. Sometimes that means having duplicates of favorite or often-used tools, but in the long run it saves so much time—time for more stitching.

▶ UP FOR GRABS

When I finish a project and have multiple fabrics left over, I tuck pieces smaller than ½ yard into large, self-sealing plastic bags, keeping the entire coordinated collection together. I can see the color families quickly when I'm looking for scraps for the next project. I store these under my cutting table in stackable shelving.

▶ TOSSED SALAD

So many of the things I do are strip pieced with scraps, so I naturally collect fabric left-overs from previous projects. I don't sort these by color, but rather dig through them when I'm designing a project. Try tossing them as you would a salad (without the salad dressing, please), taking out those pieces that don't work until you are pleased with the combination of fabrics.

▶ LUCKY LEFTOVERS

If I have leftover fabrics that are ½ yard or larger, I store them in color families on open shelving in my studio. I loosely wrap each leftover on an empty fabric bolt from my local quilt shop, slip the wrapped fabric off the bolt, and stack it neatly on the appropriate shelf. A one-step stepstool is handy for reaching the top shelves.

until you reach the center of the flame. Change to orange sewing thread and do a few chain stitches (about ¼") for the flame center. Using a single strand of orange sewing thread, backstitch around each flame.

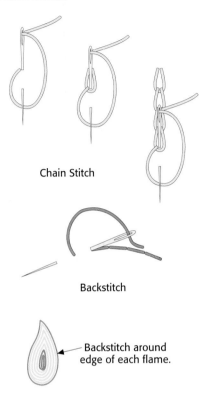

Chain Stitch

Backstitch

Backstitch around edge of each flame.

11. From fabrics #2 and #7, cut a strip 3¼" x 8½". With right sides up, lay fabric #2 over the long edge of fabric #7, leaving only 1½" of fabric #7 exposed. Use a rotary cutter to cut a softly flowing curve through both fabric layers at once. Discard the smaller pieces of fabric. Make a ¼"-long mark across both cut edges at one of the curves for matching purposes.

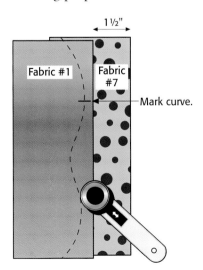

1½"

Fabric #1   Fabric #7

Mark curve.

12. With right sides together and the marks matching, pin fabric #2 to fabric #7—a bit like you would pin together the pieces of a curved patchwork block such as Drunkard's Path. Don't fret; just coax the edges together as you pin and sew ¼" from the raw edges, stitching slowly to avoid puckers. Press the seam to one side.

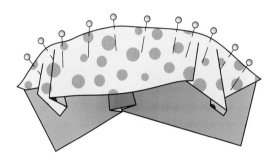

13. Use rubber stamps and permanent ink to decorate fabric #2. Tap the stamp gently on the pad to apply ink. Working on a flat, smooth surface, press the stamp firmly onto the fabric in the desired location; allow to dry thoroughly. Press from the wrong side to heat set the ink.

14. For the pieced triangle squares (right-hand border), cut 2 squares, each 2½" x 2½", from fabric #2. From fabric #7, cut one 2½" square. From fabric #3, cut three 2½" squares.

15. On the wrong side of the fabric #3 squares or the #2 and #7 squares, draw a line from one corner to the opposite corner of each square. The line is a stitching and cutting guide.

16. Place each fabric #3 square right sides together on a matching fabric #2 or fabric #7 square. Pin together and stitch ¼" away from the diagonal lines on each side.

17. Cut on the diagonal lines to make 2 pieced triangle squares from each set. Open and press the seam toward the darker fabric in each square.

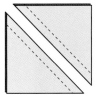 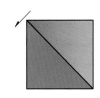

18. Referring to the quilt photo, arrange the pieced squares to create larger triangles of alternating colors. Sew the squares together and add a stamped design to one of the triangles.

19. Pin the cake section to the batting, placing it 2½" in from the right edge and centering it from top to bottom.

20. With right sides together and raw edges matching, sew the long edge of the stamped fabric and fabric #7 section to the left edge of the cake section. Stitch ¼" from the raw edges through all layers. Flip and press toward the batting and pin in place. (Use this stitch-and-flip method for the remainder of the assembly process.)

21. Couch a contrasting color accent thread in the ditch of the curved seam in the rubber-stamped section. Replace the regular presser foot on your sewing machine with a couching or zigzag foot. Place the end of the couching thread on the fabric along the seam and sew over the thread using a long, narrow zigzag stitch.

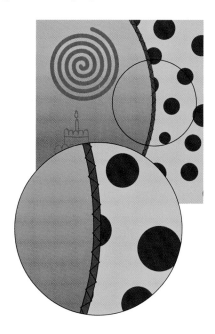

22. Cut a 1¾"-wide strip of fabric #8 and stitch and flip to the top edge of the patchwork. Cut a 2¼"-wide strip of fabric #3 and a 1¾" strip of fabric #8. Stitch and flip #3 to the left edge of the patchwork, and then add #8 to the bottom edge in the same manner. Finally, stitch and flip the strip of pieced triangle squares to the right edge. Trim as needed to "square up" the finished patchwork.

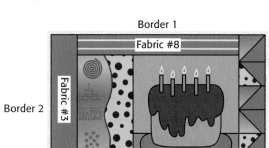

Embellishment

1. Using Templates D and E, cut D from fabric #2 and E from fabric #7. Turn under and baste ¼" on the raw edge of each circle. Hand appliqué the smaller circle above the cake and candles, inserting a 6½" length of accent thread under the bottom of the balloon and catching it in the stitching.

2. Hand appliqué the remaining circle above and to the right of cake, inserting the music button and a 6½" length of accent thread under the bottom edge of the circle.

3. Knot the 2 balloon strings together 1½" from the ends and tack to the cake.

Music button

Knot "strings" and sew to cake.

4. Sew sequins and beads to the area above the cake. Knot the thread and pass the needle up through the batting to the right side of the fabric. Slip a sequin and a seed bead onto the needle. Pass the needle down to the batting, going through the sequin only. The bead will hold the sequin to the fabric. Add more sequins and beads to the rubber-stamped area for more dazzle.

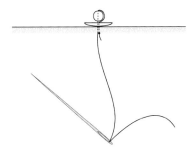

5. Add seed beads only to outline the rubber stamp designs. Attach beads to the fabric one at a time. Knot the thread and pass the needle up to the right side of the fabric. Put 1 bead on the needle and push it down the thread to the fabric. Pass the needle down through the fabric and batting close to the entering stitch. Take a small stitch on the back and bring the needle back up to the right side of the fabric. Add another bead and continue following the design. Backstitch on batting before cutting the thread at the end of the design.

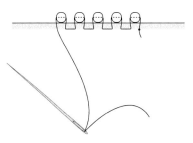

Finishing

1. Cut the backing ½" larger than the finished quilt top. Center and pin the batting and the top to the wrong side of the backing.

2. Machine quilt simple designs using an open-toe presser foot, if you have one, so you can see where you're going. Stitch next to each seam line and each appliqué piece. Use a simple straight stitch along curves, but change to the triple straight stitch, if available on your machine, for added emphasis along any straight seams.

Open-toe presser foot

3. Trim the batting and backing even with the quilt top, making sure all 4 edges are straight and the corners are square.

4. Cut 2 binding strips the length of the quilt and 2 binding strips the width of the quilt, making them each 1" wide.

5. Pin a short binding strip to each short edge of the quilt top *with the right side of the binding strip against the right side of the backing.* Stitch ¼" from the raw edges. Press the binding strips toward the seam allowances.

6. Turn the quilt over and draw a line on the wrong side of the binding strips *exactly* ¼" away from the quilt edge. Cut just outside this line with pinking shears.

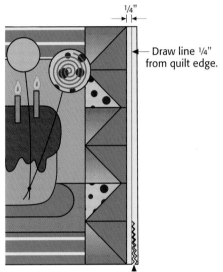

¼"

Draw line ¼" from quilt edge.

Pink to right of line.

7. Fold the binding over the seam allowance so it covers the stitching on the quilt top and pin in place. Zigzag along the pinked edge through all layers. Bind the top and bottom edges of the quilt in the same manner, using the remaining binding strips.

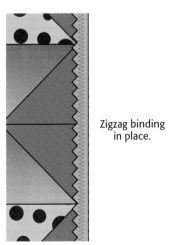

Zigzag binding in place.

8. Cut the ribbon into two 9"-long pieces and tie each in a bow. Stack and tack the bows to the upper left corner of the quilt. Sew small buttons to the remaining 3 corners.

9. Stamp a greeting on a small scrap of fabric #2. Fuse it to the wrong side of another fabric scrap. Stitch around the outside edge and trim close to the stitching. Glue or fuse to the quilt just below the cake plate (see quilt photo).

10. For a label, cut a large circle using Template F. Sign it and date it with indelible ink. Turn under ¼" all around and press. Appliqué to the back of the quilt.

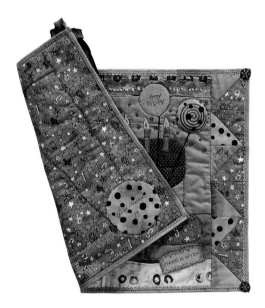

Decorate an envelope and pop this sentimental greeting card inside; then mail it to the next lucky person on your birthday card list! Won't they be surprised—and pleased—to have a piece of your clever birthday cake to keep forever!

Happy Birthday
Patterns

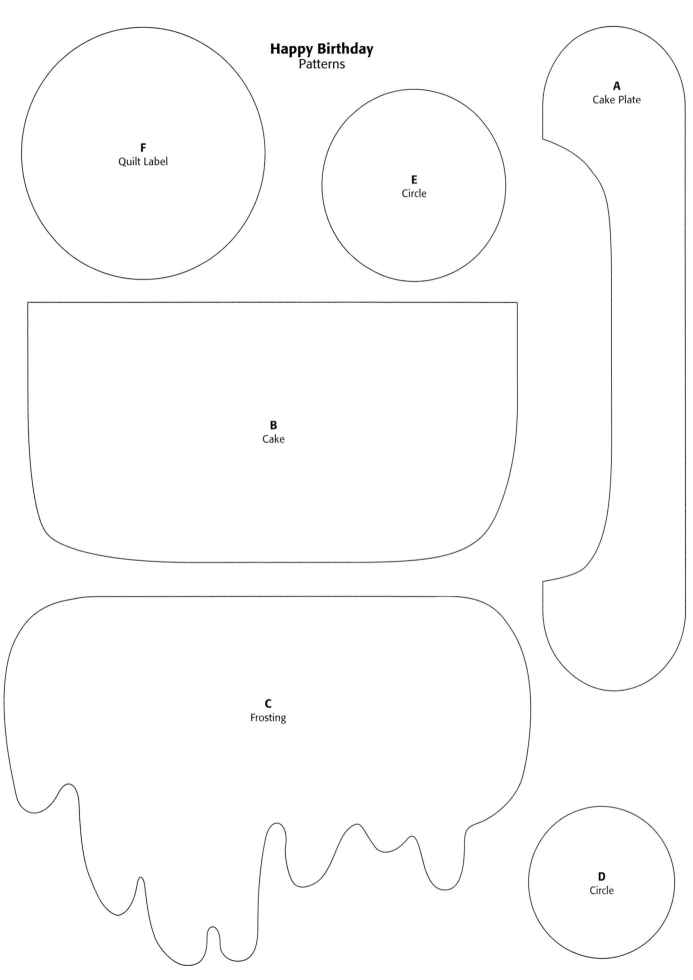

A
Cake Plate

F
Quilt Label

E
Circle

B
Cake

C
Frosting

D
Circle

Happy Anniversary

Happy Anniversary, 10" x 14", Judy Murrah, March 1999, Victoria, Texas.

I made this love note for my husband to celebrate our thirty-third wedding anniversary. It has found a home on an antique trunk in his study. Customize the directions to turn this into a greeting designed specifically for the recipient.

Materials

- ➤ Assorted fabric scraps in 8 different, coordinating colors for patchwork and binding; refer to the photo for ideas
- ➤ 10" x 14" piece of fabric for backing
- ➤ 10" x 14" piece of batting for foundation
- ➤ Photo transfer paper (the correct type for your computer printer) for word transfer

- ➤ Decorative thread, textured yarns, or ribbon for couching
- ➤ Charms, beads, and buttons for embellishment
- ➤ Bias tape maker
- ➤ ¼"-wide bias tape (optional)

Note: *All seam allowances are ¼" wide, unless otherwise noted.*

Use the patterns on page 46 to make templates.

Block 1: Radiant Star

1. From fabric #1, cut 4 squares, each 2" x 2", for the center of the square. Cut a 5" square from the same fabric. Fold the 5" square in half diagonally, and then in half again. Press and unfold.

2. From each of fabrics #2, #3, and #4, cut 8 squares, each 2" x 2", for a total of 24 squares.

3. Fold each of the 2" squares of fabric #1 in half with wrong sides together and press. Fold corners C and D to the center to make a triangle. Press. Repeat with squares of fabrics #2, #3, and #4. Each group of squares will make 1 round of points on the star.

4. Decide the order in which you want to use the fabrics. The star shows up best when rows are arranged in contrasting values of light and dark. Position the 4 innermost triangles on the right side of the creased 5" square so the points meet in the center and line up with the creases. Pin in place. Tack the points in place at the center with a stitch in the fold from one point to the point opposite it. Come up to the top again and stitch in the other fold from one point to the opposite point. Machine stitch the outer raw edges of the triangles through all layers. This makes the center of the star.

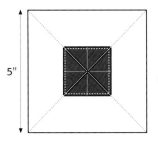

Tack in center of 5" square.

5. Arrange the 8 triangles of the next color with their points ¼" from the center and directly in line with the points of the 4 innermost triangles. Position the triangles in a clockwise fashion so the raw edges overlap in a consistent direction. Tack the tips in place with matching thread and machine stitch the raw edges through all layers.

6. Tack and stitch the triangles for the remaining 2 rounds of star points in the same manner. When the star is complete, you will have an octagon shape on the background square.

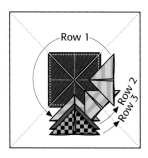

Triangles form an octagon.

7. Position a tracing of Template A on top of the completed star with the raw edges of the outer round of star points extending at least ¼" beyond the outer edge of the template. Adjust the template size as needed.

8. Cut two 5½" squares from fabric #5. Center the circle template on the wrong side of one of the 5½" squares and draw around it. Place the 2 squares right sides together with all raw edges even. Using a short stitch length, sew around the circle through both layers.

9. Carefully cut out the circle center through both layers, leaving a ⅛"-wide seam allowance all around. Clip the seam allowance to the stitching, spacing clips every ¼" around the circle. Set the circle cutouts aside to use for 2 Yo-Yos.

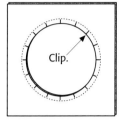 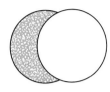

Save circles.

10. Turn the piece right side out and press along the seam edge. Center the folded star behind the opening in the square. Lift up the upper square and pin the lower square to the star. Stitch around the first stitching line to attach the window to the star. No stitching will show on the right side.

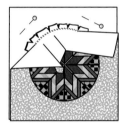

11. Press the star. Stitch ⅛" from the raw edges.

12. Pin the completed star block in the lower left corner of the piece of batting.

Block 2: Cross My Heart

SEE PAGE 46 for optional words to use for photo transfers.

1. Cut a 2" x 10" strip each of fabrics #2 and #3. On the lighter of fabrics #2 and #3, mark 2" intervals on the wrong side. These will be cutting lines later. Draw a line from one corner to the opposite corner of each marked square. These are stitching and cutting guides.

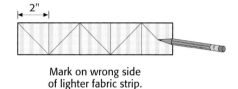

Mark on wrong side
of lighter fabric strip.

2. Pin the fabric #2 and fabric #3 strips right sides together. Stitch ¼" away from the diagonal lines on each side, taking 1 stitch over the raw edge and then pivoting the strip so you can stitch the entire piece on one side of the line without stopping. Repeat for the other side of the line.

Stitch ¼" away from diagonal line
in a zigzag manner.

3. Cut into 5 squares on the vertical lines. Cut the squares along the lines between the rows of stitching for a total of 10 pieced squares. Press the seams toward the darker fabric in each square. Trim off the ¼" ears that extend beyond the block.

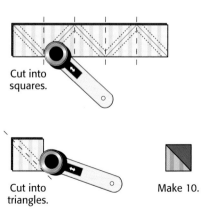

Cut into
squares.

Cut into
triangles.

Make 10.

4. Cut a 1¾" x 16" strip of fabric #6. Cut the strip into 1¾" squares. Apply photo transfer words to the squares. You may choose to use words from page 46. Follow the photo transfer directions on your package of transfer paper.

5. Arrange the pieced squares in 3 sections as shown, experimenting with the patterns you can make. Add 1¾" squares to fill in the design. Sew each section together, but do not sew the sections to each other. Press seams in direction of arrows.

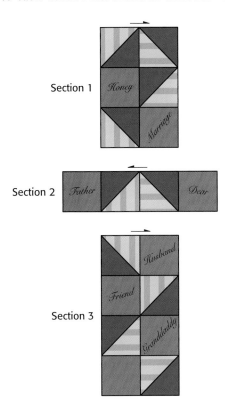

6. With right sides together, stitch section 3 to the star block. Flip onto the batting and press. Set the other sections to the side for now.

Block 3: Bordered Prairie Points

1. Cut 2 rectangles, each 2" x 4", of fabric #4 and 2 rectangles, each 2½" x 4", of fabric #1. With right sides together, sew the long edge of rectangles of 2 different fabrics together. Press the seam toward fabric #1, and then press the 2 wrong sides

together with ¼" fabric #1 showing at the finished edge above fabric #4.

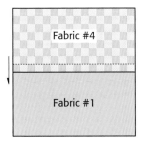

2. Fold each short end to the center, as for the square in Radiant Star (page 39). Press. Set aside.

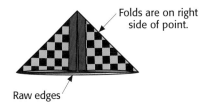

Folds are on right side of point.

Raw edges

Block 4: The Path of Love

1. Pin two 4½" squares of fabric #5 right sides together. Cut a curved line through the center of the squares.

Wrong side

2 layers of Fabric #5

2. Stitch the matching sections together ¼" from the cut edges. Clip curves. Turn both pieces right side out. Press.

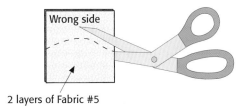

3. Position a 2" x 4½" rectangle of fabric #1 on the batting and place the cut-and-stitched curved pieces on top. Adjust until you are pleased with the appearance. Carefully remove the layered pieces from the batting and topstitch the curved pieces to fabric #1 only.

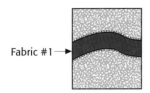

Fabric #1 ──→

4. Stitch and flip the block to the right edge of section 3 of Cross My Heart.

5. Stitch and flip a strip of fabric #2 that is wide enough to cover the remainder of the batting to the right edge of the path block.

6. Add 1¾"-wide strips of fabric #2 to each end of section 2 of Cross My Heart so it will reach to the edges of the batting (cut it extra long and trim even with batting after stitching). Stitch and flip section 2 to section 3, matching seam allowances.

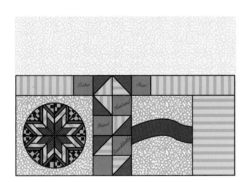

Block 5: Love Note Pocket

1. Cut 2 of Template B from fabric #5. Cut 2 of Template C from fabric #3.

2. With right sides facing, sew the 2 fabric #5 layers together, leaving an opening for turning. Clip curves. Turn right side out. Repeat with the fabric #3 layers. Blanket stitch the top edge of the fabric #3 piece.

3. Position the fabric #5 piece on top of the fabric #3 piece with round edges even. Machine or hand stitch with blanket stitch to hold the 2 pieces together along the curved edge.

4. Add a button and/or snap to hold the flap to the front of the pocket. Write a love note and tuck it in the pocket.

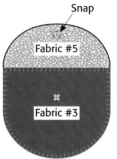

Snap

Fabric #5

Fabric #3

Blanket stitch edges together.

5. Center the little pocket on a 4½" x 5½" rectangle of fabric # 1; pin in place. Stitch close to the outer curved edge. With right sides together, stitch the 4½" x 5½" rectangle to the left edge of section 1 of Cross My Heart.

Block 6: Yo-Yos

1. With right sides together, stitch a 3" x 4¼" piece of fabric #1 to the right edge of section 1 of Cross My Heart. You will add Yo-Yos to this piece later.

2. To make the gathered Yo-Yo, thread a needle, double the thread, and knot the ends together. Turn under ⅛" at the edge of a circle cutout left from the Radiant Star block (pages 39–40) and sew a running stitch very close to the folded edge. Draw up the thread as tightly as possible to form a tight circle. Primp the circle so the hole is in the center. Bring the needle to the back side and backstitch to secure. Set aside.

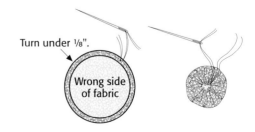

Turn under ⅛".

Wrong side of fabric

3. For a folded Yo-Yo, fold the circle in half, then in half again to find the center. Finger press to make a crease.

4. Fold the bottom of the circle to the center. Crease and tack with thread. Continue folding and bringing the right-hand corner to the center until there are 6 even folds. Tack to the center after each fold with 1 stitch, catching all points. Set aside.

Block 7: Origami Bow Tie

YOU'LL HAVE to trust me on this! Follow each step carefully so that you end up with a folded, three-dimensional knot in the center of the pieced block.

1. Cut 3 squares, each 2" x 2", of fabric #3 and 2 squares, each 2" x 2", of fabric #6. Fold one of the fabric #3 bow-tie squares in half, wrong sides together. This square will be the center of the tie. Place the folded square on the right side of one of the fabric #6 background squares so the fold runs horizontally through the center of the background square and the raw edges are even on the lower right edge.

Fabric #6

Fabric #3

2. With right sides together and raw edges even, place a #3 bow-tie square on top of the first 2 pieces. Pin the pieces and stitch along the right edge, catching the short end of the folded square in the seam.

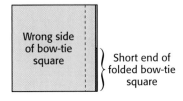

Wrong side of bow-tie square

Short end of folded bow-tie square

3. Fold the bow-tie square and the background square away from the folded square.

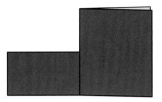

4. Place a #6 background square right side up and position the remaining short end of the folded square on top with raw edges even.

5. Place a #3 bow-tie square on top of the short end of the folded square with right sides together and raw edges even; pin. Stitch along the left edge, catching the short end of the folded square in the seam. Fold the bow-tie square and the background square away from the folded square.

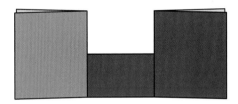

6. Open out the center folded square and place the raw edges together, matching seams at the center (wrong sides of the square will be together). Pin the layers together with the bow-tie square sandwiched between and the seams in opposite directions. Stitch across the squares, catching the folded square in the seam.

Dotted lines indicate position of folded layers.

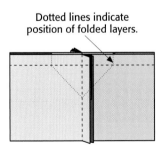

7. Open the squares away from the center. Press.

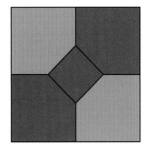

8. Sew the bow-tie square to the right edge of the Yo-Yo square. Add a piece of fabric #1 to the right edge of the bow tie so that the finished piece of patchwork will be 14¼" long. Press seams in one direction.

9. With right sides together, pin the strip of patchwork to the top edge of the pieces already attached to the foundation. Make sure to match the seam lines of the Cross My Heart rows. Stitch and flip. Press. Referring to the photo for placement, pin the Prairie Points, folded side up, to the right edge of the love note. Position and stitch Yo-Yos to the background fabric next to the bow-tie square. Trim the edges of patchwork even with batting as needed.

Finishing

1. Couch over decorative thread, textured yarns, or ribbon to outline Cross My Heart. Use an all-purpose sewing foot or cording foot (or a couching or braiding foot). Stitch over the threads from the top with another thread, using a regular zigzag setting. Adjust the zigzag width to just clear the width of the decorative yarn or thread you will stitch over.

2. To begin, pull about 2" of yarn behind the foot and begin to stitch, zigzagging over the yarn, holding it taut in front of the foot. The needle and presser foot will do the work as you keep the yarn centered under the foot. If your machine has a couching or braiding foot, use it. It holds the yarn in front of the foot, freeing your hands for maneuvering the fabric.

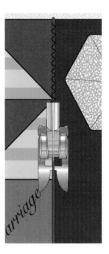

3. Pin the patchwork/foundation face up on the wrong side of the backing with raw edges even. Stitch ⅛" from the outside edge. Embellish with beads, quilting, buttons, and charms as desired.

4. For the outer bias, cut 1¼"-wide bias strips from fabric #8. Cut ½"-wide bias strips from fabric #7 for the inner bias (added last). Join each set of strips to make a piece of each that is 54" long. You may also use purchased ¼"-wide bias tape for the inner bias.

5. Pin the right side of the 1¼"-wide bias to the backing side of the love note with raw edges even. Stitch ¼" from the raw edges, mitering corners as shown.

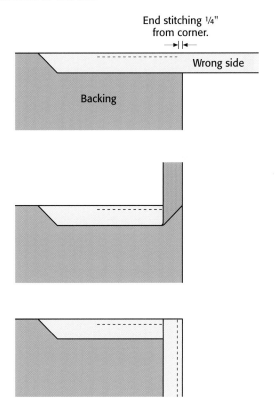

End stitching ¼" from corner.

Wrong side

Backing

6. Turn the bias to the right side of the quilt, encasing the raw edges. Pin the bias in place, folding in the mitered corners. It's not necessary to turn under the raw edge of the bias on the right side. Stitch in the ditch of the seam on the backing side to catch the raw edge in place on the right side.

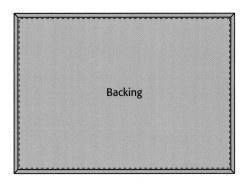

Backing

7. Use a bias-tape maker to make ¼"-wide finished bias tape from the ½"-wide strips of fabric. Or fold unfinished long edges of bias to wrong side center. Press.

8. Using the machine stitching on the flat bias binding as a guide, position the prepared or purchased bias strip over the raw edges of the bias binding. Pin in place, mitering the corners. Stitch close to both edges.

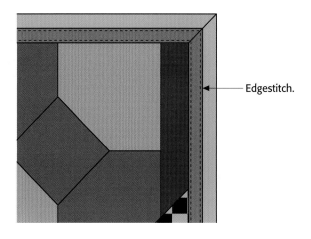

Edgestitch.

Happy anniversary, honey!

> **DESIGNER TIP**
When making love notes, I think about the recipient and things or memories that have meaning for both of us. I incorporate these things into this expression of love.

Happy Anniversary
Patterns

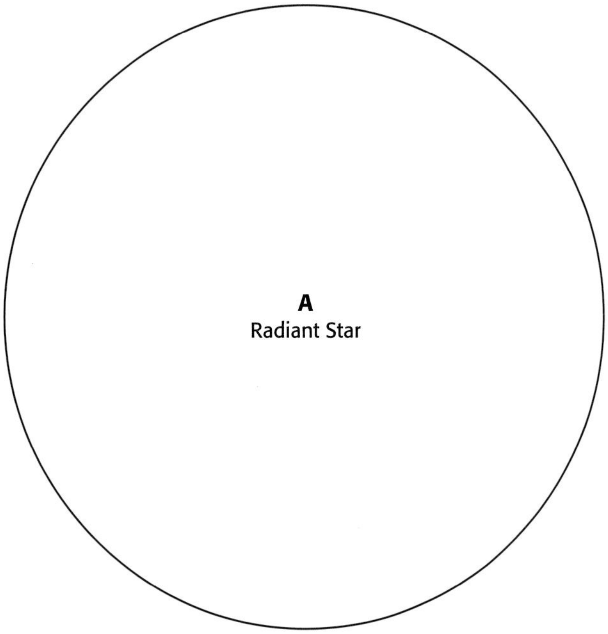

A
Radiant Star

Fold line

B
Love Note Pocket

C
Love Note Pocket

Angel

Baby

Bride

Brother

Daughter

Dear

Family

Father

Friend

Granddaddy

Grammy

Groom

Home

Honey

Husband

Love

Marriage

Mother

Sister

Son

Sweetheart

Wife

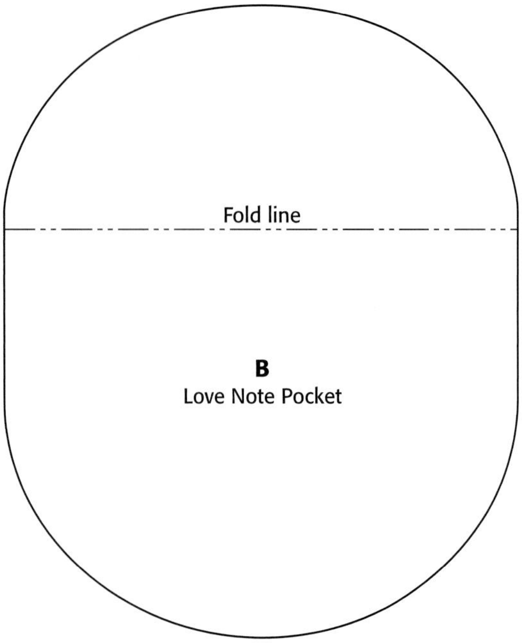

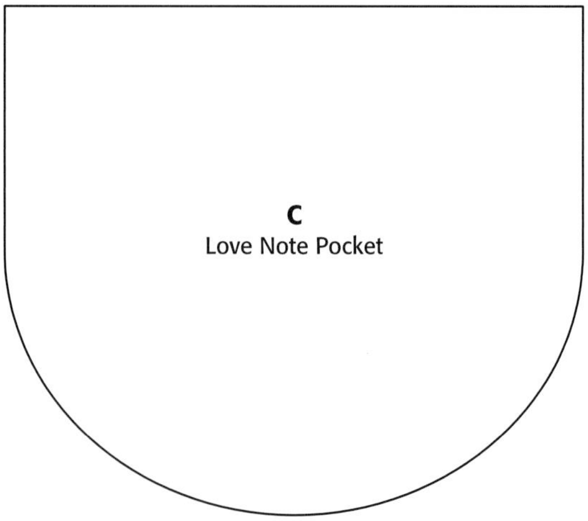

PART TWO

PLAYING WITH QUILTS

Most of my quilts start with strips of fabric, leftover piecing, or squares that were cut for another project but not used. I simply sew strips together, cut them at an angle, and sew them back together again in a different combination. I join pieces leftover from this process with something else to create another section of a patchwork piece. This creates the "canvas," and then the embellishing begins.

Not Your Everyday Sampler

Not Your Everyday Sampler, 39½" x 49½", Judy Murrah, March 2000, Victoria, Texas.

Although the inspiration for this quilt was the design on the lid of a shoebox, the only thing the quilt and shoebox really share in common is that they each have twelve blocks! The quilt is a good example of how someone else's art can spur you to try a new approach to your own art.

Use the patterns on pages 57–58 to make Templates A–L.

Block 1: Beribboned Heart

> **➤ DESIGNER TIP**
> If you're a teacher, you can teach this quilt as a block-of-the-month class. If you're doing this quilt on your own, consider stitching with a fellow quilting friend once a month to learn the techniques in each block together. (Perhaps you can share fabric leftovers, too!) I save space on my calendar for "play days" several times throughout the year so I can share the good times with a friend who shares my passions.

Materials

➤ Assorted fabric scraps in colors that work well together for patchwork

➤ ⅓ yd. fabric for bias binding

➤ ⅛ yd. each of 3 different fabrics in similar colors for pieced sashing #1★

➤ ⅛ yd. each of 2 fabrics in similar colors for pieced sashing #2★

➤ Leftover piecing from previous projects for "flags" border

➤ 1¾ yds. backing fabric

➤ 44" x 57" batting for foundation

➤ 14"-long piece of ½"-wide ribbon for Block #1

➤ Steam-A-Seam 2 (or other transfer paper–backed fusible web of your choice)

➤ Assorted ribbon scraps for embellishment

➤ Sulky Tear-Easy stabilizer

➤ Buttons, beads, and trinkets for embellishment

➤ #8 perle cotton thread for ties

➤ Various threads for machine quilting

➤ 5 yds. decorative trim for outside edge

★*It's best to choose these fabrics after you have completed your blocks.*

1. Sew assorted strips and pieces of fabric together to make a 9½" x 9½" random-pieced square.

2. Trace the large heart (Template A) on the right side of a piece of fabric. Cut out ¼" beyond the drawn line. Turn under ¼" all around and baste. Pin to the center of the pieced block.

3. Cut leaves B and C from chosen fabrics. Fold each leaf shape in half lengthwise with right sides together and stitch ⅛" from the long raw edge. Clip off tip and flatten with seam at center back. Turn right side out.

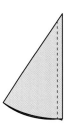

4. Using doubled matching thread and starting at the tip, hand baste along the center of each leaf as shown. Tug on the thread gently to slightly gather the leaf. Backstitch to secure and clip the thread. Gather the bottom raw edge of the leaf in the same manner.

Finished leaf

5. Pin the wide end of each leaf under the heart. Hand appliqué the heart and leaves in place.

6. Fold the ½"-wide ribbon in half crosswise and pinch it at the fold. Stitch the layers together 2" from the fold. Sew to the top of the heart with small hand stitches. Sew the ends of the ribbon (cut on the bias) to the block. Allow a little extra ease in each length for added softness and drape.

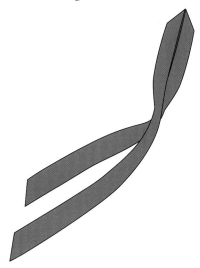

7. For the fabric rose, cut a 14"- to 16"-long strip of bias from the chosen fabric, making it 4" wide at one end and tapering to 2" wide at the opposite end. Fold the strip in half lengthwise with wrong sides together and raw edges even; pin. Press lightly if desired or leave unpressed for a softer flower.

8. Machine baste the raw edges together. Draw up the basting thread tightly to gather. Beginning at the narrow end, roll the strip into flower; hand sew the basted edges together as you roll.

Bias flower

9. When you reach the end, fold the edge under and stitch it to the bottom of the flower. Hand sew the flower in place on the beribboned heart.

Stitch end of strip
to flower bottom.

10. Trace around Template D on Steam-A-Seam 2 backing paper. Remove the other backing paper and apply the fusible web to the wrong side of a fabric scrap. Cut out the heart, peel away the remaining backing paper, and fuse the heart to the block (see photo for placement). Machine appliqué in place.

NOTE: *Steam-A-Seam 2 has fusible web sandwiched between 2 sheets of backing paper. Check to see which liner removes first by peeling apart at the corner. Trace on the sheet that will be left behind.*

Block 2: Perky Pyramids

1. Cut a 15"-long strip from each of 4 different fabrics, cutting 2 strips 1½" wide and 2 strips 1¾" wide. Sew the strips together, alternating the 2 widths, to make a 5" x 15" strip-pieced unit. Press the seams in one direction. Repeat, using different but coordinating fabrics and these widths: 1½", 1¾", 2", and 1¼". Sew together the second set of strips in the order given.

2. Using Template E, cut 5 triangles from each of the strip units from step 1.

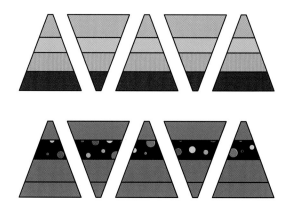

3. Alternating the triangles, arrange and sew them together in 2 rows. Sew the 2 rows together.

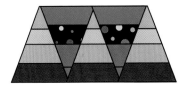

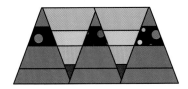

4. Trim the unit to 7½" x 9½".

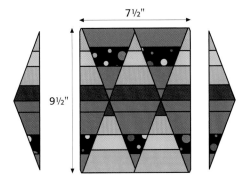

5. Add a 2½" x 9½" scrap strip to one long edge of the block to make it a 9½" square.

Block 3: Fandango

1. Use Template F to mark 10 fan blades on a variety of fabric scraps. Cut out on the drawn lines.

2. Cut an 8" square from a fabric scrap for the fan background. Create a fan by arranging the fan blades on top of the background square in the order desired. Remove the blades from the background square. Stitch the blades together and press the seams in one direction.

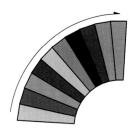

3. Position the fan diagonally across the background square and stitch ⅛" from the upper and lower raw edges. Cover the raw edges with narrow bias tape. Stitch in place along both edges.

4. Cover the upper corner of the block with strips of fabric and ribbon if desired and embellish with a machine-appliquéd heart as described for Block 1 in step 10 on page 50.

5. To make the rose, use Template G to cut 1 circle from each of 2 different fabrics. Make a ¾"-long slit in the center of the circle you want on top. Pin circles right sides together and stitch them together ¼" from the raw edge. Turn right side out through the slit and press.

Turn right side out through slit.

6. Cut several ¼" x 3" strips from 3 different fabrics. Fold the strips in half crosswise in a bunch and tuck the folded end into the slit in the circle. Tack the strips to the circle. Hand baste the opening to the strips and the back of the circle and draw up the stitches tightly to ruffle the circle. Backstitch. Appliqué the center of the completed flower to the fan.

7. Add a strip of fabric of your choice to the side and bottom edges of the block to make a 9½" square block.

Block 4: Wacky Four Patch

1. From each of 2 fabrics, cut a 1½" x 4" strip. Sew the 2 strips together and press the seam toward the darker of the 2 strips. Cut 2 segments, each 1½" wide.

2. Sew the 2 segments together as shown and press the seam in one direction.

3. Now the fun begins—there are no rules. Add strips of fabric and leftover patchwork strips around the four-patch unit, working clockwise or counterclockwise, Log-Cabin style. Use a variety of strip widths and shapes so the Four Patch will end up off center and askew in the finished block. Keep adding strips until the block measures 8¼" square. You may need to trim to that size. Add a strip of fabric to the right and bottom edges of the block to make it 9½" square.

Block 5: Do the Reverse

1. Choose 2 fabrics, each 6" x 9½", for this double-layer block. For the top layer, choose a solid color or a tone-on-tone print. For the bottom layer, choose a print with motifs that you can see from the wrong side so that you can stitch around selected ones.

2. Cut a 6" x 9½" piece of Steam-A-Seam 2 fusible web and apply it to the wrong side of the top fabric layer. Remove the transfer-paper backing.

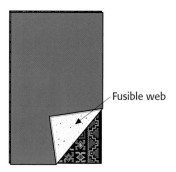

Fusible web

3. Place the top layer right side up on the right side of the bottom layer and pin the layers together. *Do not fuse.* With the bottom fabric wrong side up, stitch around the selected motifs.

4. Cut away the top layer of fabric inside the stitched shapes so the bottom fabric shows through. Be sure to trim close to the stitching.

5. After all shapes are trimmed, fuse the 2 layers together following the manufacturer's directions.

6. Add strips of fabric to the right and left sides to make a 9½" square.

Block 6: Mardi Gras!

1. Cut an 8¾" square of fabric for the block background. Place it on top of a matching piece of Sulky Tear-Easy stabilizer. Pin layers together.

2. Stick Steam-A-Seam 2 fusible web to the wrong side of several small scraps of assorted fabrics. Draw geometric shapes on the remaining transfer paper, and then cut out. Remove the transfer paper.

3. Arrange the shapes on the right side of the fabric square with stabilizer underneath. Apply pressure to stick the fabric shapes in place. If you are using a fusible web other than Steam-A-Seam 2, fuse the shapes in place before proceeding. Stitch around each shape, using a variety of stitches including triple straight stitch, zigzagging, free-motion stitching, and couching. Use a variety of threads for added interest.

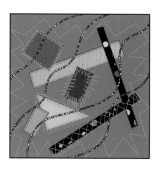

4. Add fabric strips to the bottom and right edges of the square to make a 9½" square.

Block 7: Pinwheel Magic

1. For the large center pinwheel, cut four 2½" x 4½" rectangles from 1 fabric. Cut four 2½" squares from each of 2 fabrics for a total of 8 squares.

2. On the wrong side of the small squares, draw a diagonal line from one corner to the opposite one.

3. With right sides together, place a square on one end of a rectangle. Stitch on the marked line. Cut ¼" from the seam. Press the seam toward the rectangle. Repeat with a square cut from different fabric on the other end of the rectangle.

Make 4.

4. Repeat steps 3 and 4 with the remaining squares for a total of 4 identical units.

5. From a contrasting fabric, cut 4 rectangles, each 2½" x 4½". Sew 1 to each triangle unit.

6. Arrange the 4 units and sew together to create a square. Press seams in direction of arrows.

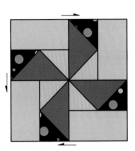

7. Add fabric strips to the top and left edges of the square to make it 9½" square.

Block 8: Colorful Courthouse

1. Cut a 2" square for the block center and cut two 1¼"-wide strips from each of 10 different fabric scraps. The longest strips should be 20" long and the shortest should be 4". The others should increase by approximately 4" per pair.

2. Sew strip #1 to one edge of the square and press the seam toward the strip. Trim even with the square. Repeat on the opposite edge of the square. Add strip #2 to the remaining edges of the square and press in the same fashion.

3. Continue adding strips in this manner until you have added a pair cut from each fabric. Trim the block to 9½" square if necessary.

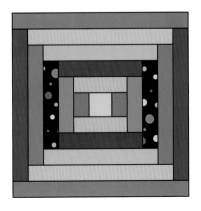

Block 9: With Heart in Hand

1. Cut one 8" x 9" piece of fabric for the block background.

2. Trace Templates H and I on a piece of Steam-A-Seam 2. Cut the shapes apart, leaving a margin all around each shape. Peel away one layer of paper and stick the Steam-A-Seam 2 shapes to the wrong side of 2 contrasting fabrics. Cut out the shapes on the lines.

3. Using Template J, trace a heart onto the center of the hand. Carefully cut out the heart with very sharp scissors and set aside to appliqué later.

4. Position the large heart on the block background (see photo) and fuse in place. Add the hand, making sure to position it so the background fabric shows through the cutout area. Fuse in place. Fuse the small heart to the background in the corner to the left of the large one. Machine appliqué each shape to the background fabric.

5. Embellish the large heart and the cutout in the hand by outlining them with buttons and beads. Sew a bead just below the inner point of the small heart appliqué.

6. Add fabric strips to the top and right edges of the block to make it 9½" square.

Block 10: Strippy Scraps

1. Cut 1½" wide pieces of assorted scraps in assorted lengths (none longer than 2") and sew them together, end to end, to make a 70"-long piece.

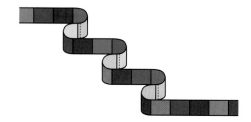

2. Make a 60" x 1" strip in the same manner. Use slightly longer pieces cut from fabric scraps that are lighter in color than those in the first strip.

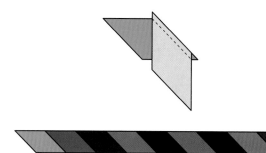

3. Cut both strips into 9" lengths, and then sew the strips together alternating the wide and narrow strips. Press the seams in one direction. Add a fabric strip to the bottom edge of the block to make it 9½" square. Trim if needed.

Block 11: Diamond Delight

1. Trace Template K to cut 22 diamonds from a variety of fabrics.

2. Arrange the diamonds in a row, short end to short end, and sew them together to make one long strip. Press the seams in one direction.

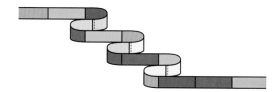

3. Cut the diamond strip into 5 equal segments. Sew the rows together to make a piece that is approximately 7½" x 8½". Press the seams in one direction. Trim the piece so all edges are straight and at right angles to each other. Add a strip of fabric to the left and bottom edges of the block to make it 9½" square.

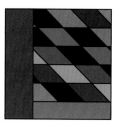

Block 12: Triangles Squared

1. Choose 5 different fabrics. Cut one 1½" x 11" strip each from fabrics #1, #2, and #4. Cut an additional 1" x 11" strip from fabric #2. Cut one 1¼" x 11" strip each from fabrics #3 and #5.

2. Sew the strips together in numerical order (the 1½" x 11" fabric #2 strip should fall after fabric #5) and press the seams in one direction. Using Template L, cut 4 triangles from the pieced unit.

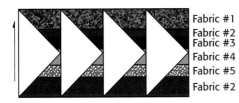

3. Sew the triangles together in pairs to make two 3½" squares.

Make 2.

4. Choose 3 fabrics for the four-patch units and cut 2" squares from each: 4 squares from fabric #1 and 2 squares from each of the remaining fabrics. Following the illustration below, arrange the squares and sew into 2 four-patch units.

Make 2.

5. Sew the triangle and four-patch units together to create a 6" x 6" pieced square.

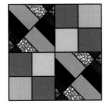

6. Stitch and flip a contrasting fabric to the top and bottom edges of the block. Press the seams toward the fabric strips. Add fabric to the right and left edges in the same manner, adding enough all around so that you can tip the block askew before trimming it to 7¾" x 9½". Add a strip to the right edge so the entire block measures 9½" square.

Quilt Top Assembly

1. Cutting across the fabric width, cut 3 strips, each 1½" wide, from each of the 3 fabrics for pieced sashing #1 (a total of 9 strips). Sew them together to create a strip-pieced unit. Press the seams in one direction. Crosscut into 1½"-wide segments and sew together to make 1 long piece of sashing.

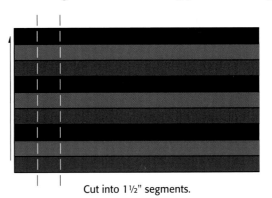

Cut into 1½" segments.

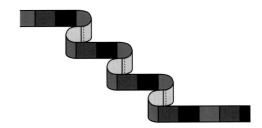

2. Repeat the process with the 2 fabrics for pieced sashing #2. You will have a longer piece of pieced sashing #1.

3. Arrange the completed blocks in rows of 3 blocks each and decide where you want to use the 2 different sashings. Cut and sew a sashing strip to the right edge of the first and second block in each row. Press the seams toward the sashing. Sew the sashed blocks together in rows. Press the seams toward the sashing.

4. Cut and sew a sashing strip to the bottom edge of the first 3 rows. Sew the rows together, and then add a sashing strip to the top and bottom edges of the quilt top, then the left and right edges.

Flags Border Assembly

NOW IT's time to play. Use up fabric scraps and your leftovers from making the 12 blocks to create patchwork pieces that each measure 4" wide—the "flags." The lengths of the flags can vary, depending on what you decide to piece together. Use some techniques you learned while piecing the blocks to create enough flags to border the quilt. See the quilt photo on page 48 for ideas.

1. Arrange and stitch the flags together along the 4" edges to make border strips long enough for the top and bottom edges of the quilt. Sew them in place and press the seams toward the borders.

2. Repeat for the left and right edges of the quilt.

3. Hang your quilt and study each of the blocks. Embellish as desired with buttons, trinkets, beads, and so on. You can always add more embellishment after the quilt is completed.

Finishing

1. Cut the backing and batting 2" larger all around than the quilt top. Layer the quilt top with the batting and backing.

2. Tie the layers together in several places to hold them together for machine quilting. These little ties will remain in the finished quilt, so use a coordinating color (or colors) of thread. Make a single stitch through all layers, leaving a 3" tail at both ends. Tie the tails in a square knot close to the surface of the quilt. Don't pull the thread too tightly or it will create a pucker. Trim both thread tails to ½"–¾" long.

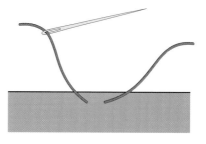

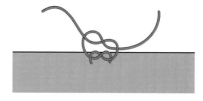

3. Machine quilt as desired.

4. Sew the binding to the wrong side of the quilt; then wrap it to the front. Fold under the raw edge, pin in place, and stitch from the front, just along the folded edge, to secure the binding edge.

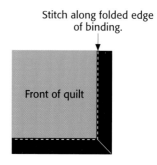

5. Position trim over the binding edge on the right side of the quilt and stitch in place.

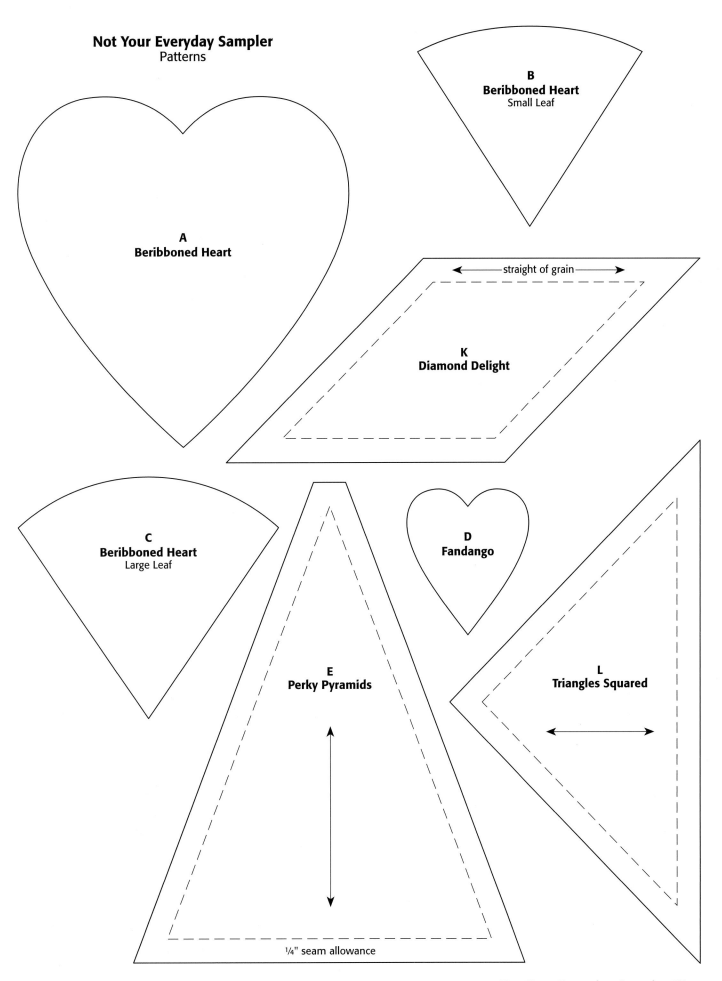

Not Your Everyday Sampler
Patterns

A
Beribboned Heart

B
Beribboned Heart
Small Leaf

straight of grain

K
Diamond Delight

C
Beribboned Heart
Large Leaf

E
Perky Pyramids

D
Fandango

L
Triangles Squared

¼" seam allowance

Not Your Everyday Sampler
Patterns

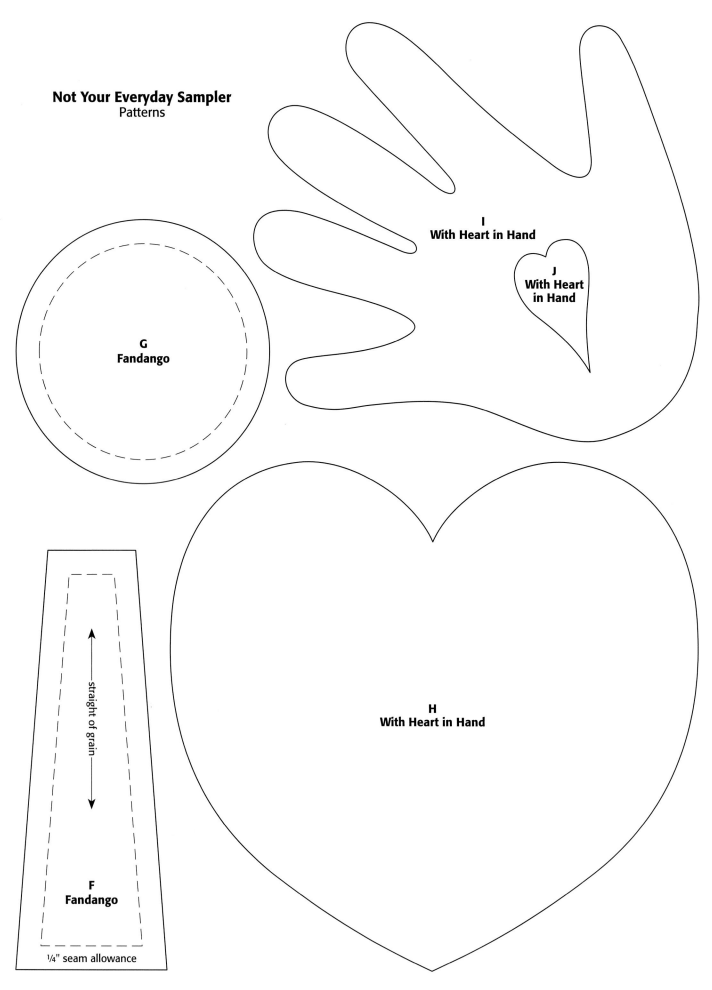

G
Fandango

I
With Heart in Hand

J
With Heart
in Hand

straight of grain

F
Fandango

¼" seam allowance

H
With Heart in Hand

Sliced Lightning

Sliced Lightning, 32" x 46", Judy Murrah, February 2000, Victoria, Texas.

Bright and easy—that's what this quilt is. You'll need quarter-yard cuts of several fabrics in each of two coordinating color families. The piecing is easier than it looks—simply piece fourteen fabric strips together and slice as directed, adding strip dividers and corner triangles to make each block. It's easy to stitch and slice your way to a bed-size quilt if you prefer—just make more blocks following these easy steps.

Materials

- ⅛ yd. each of 7 fabrics in color #1 for patchwork
- ⅛ yd. each of 7 fabrics in color #2 for patchwork
- ½ yd. fabric #1 for triangles
- 1¼ yds. fabric #2 for dividing strips, inner border, and backing
- ⅓ yd. fabric #3 for binding
- 36" x 50" piece of batting for foundation
- 9½" square ruler by Omnigrid

Note: *All seam allowances are ¼" wide..*

Use the patterns on page 63 to make Templates A and B.

For a scrappy version of this quilt, choose a variety of fabrics from your stash and cut 28 strips, each 1½" wide, cutting across the fabric width.

Block Assembly

1. Cut two 1½"-wide strips from each fabric in each of the 2 colors—a total of 28 strips, each 42" to 44" long. (If using fat quarters or scraps, piece strips so that they are 42" to 44" long before continuing with the following steps.)

2. Alternating strips from each of the 2 colors (or contrasting colors for a scrap quilt), sew 14 different strips together. Repeat with the remaining strips to make a second piece, varying the order of the strips from the first. Press all seams in one direction in each strip-pieced unit.

3. From each strip-pieced unit, cut six 6½"-wide pieces (a total of 12 pieces). Save the remainder of each strip-pieced unit to use in the outer border.

NOTE: *Every second or third cut, check the ruler position to make sure that you are making "square cuts." Trim the cut edge as necessary to keep the ruler edge and seam lines perpendicular to each other.*

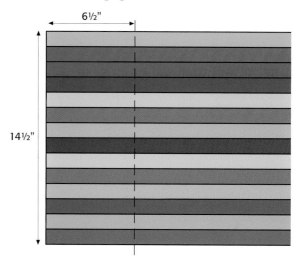

4. On the 9½"-square ruler, place a piece of masking tape at the 4⅞" diagonal of 2 opposite corners as shown.

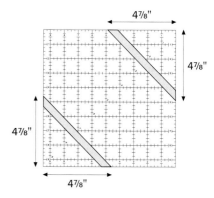

5. Position the ruler on one of the strip-pieced sections with the tape edge positioned at the top and bottom edges. Center the ruler on the section from left to right.

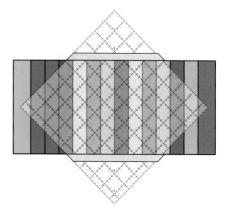

6. Cut off the 4 corners of the section that extend beyond the ruler edges. Repeat with the remaining 11 sections. Set aside the cutaway corners for the outer border.

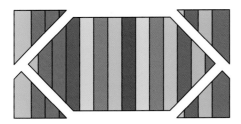

7. From fabric #1, cut 3 strips, each 4¼" wide. Using Template A, cut a total of 24 triangles from the strips, flipping the triangle position with each cut. If you have a ruler you can adapt to this triangle size, use it for easier rotary cutting.

Template A

8. Sew a triangle to each long side of each strip-pieced segment to make twelve 9½" squares. Press seams toward the triangles. Square up with a rotary cutter and ruler, if necessary.

9. Slice each square diagonally across the strip piecing. Keep the pieces together in matching pairs.

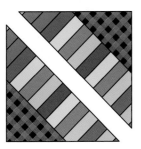

10. From fabric # 2, cut 4 strips each 1" wide, cutting across the fabric width. Cut each strip into 3 equal lengths for a total of 12 strips.

11. Join each matching pair of triangles with one strip, making sure that the strips extend an equal amount beyond the triangle ends. Press the seams toward the strip and trim excess at block corners.

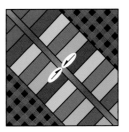

Quilt Top Assembly

1. Referring to the quilt photo and the illustration on page 62, arrange the blocks in 4 rows of 3 blocks each so that you create "lightning bolts" running the length of the quilt top. Sew together in rows and press the seams in opposite directions from row to row.

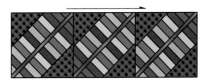

Rows 1 and 3

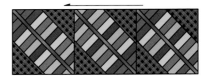

Rows 2 and 4

NOTE: *The corners of the triangles are slightly offset where they meet at each seam.*

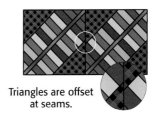

Triangles are offset at seams.

Assembly

1. Layer the three 7½" x 9½" fabric strips right side up, placing the brightest fabric on top. Pin the layers together to secure them for stitching.

    NOTE: *You will wash and dry the stack after stitching and slashing. The cut edges will fray, and the colors will soften somewhat.*

2. Stitch through all 3 layers of fabric in rows parallel to or on a diagonal to the long side of the strip. Without breaking the thread, pivot the fabric and stitch back to the side on which you started, spacing stitching rows approximately ¼" apart to create channels for cutting.

> **DESIGNER TIP**
> The closer to the true-bias grain the stitching runs, the less fraying you will get after cutting the channels and washing the piece. The closer it is to the straight of grain, the more fraying there will be along the cut edges. Fraying gives a fuzzier, softer look.

3. Using a small, sharp pair of scissors and starting at a raw edge, cut through *only the top 2 layers of fabric* in every stitching channel. *Be careful not to cut through the bottom layer of fabric.* Alternatively, you can use the Slash Cutter by Clover to make cutting quicker and easier than it is with the scissors.

4. After slashing each channel, wet the piece and put it in a dryer with other items. When it is completely dry, remove it from the dryer and shake to remove loose threads. You may need to trim excess threads away.

5. From the completed chenille, cut 2 pieces, each 4½" x 7".

6. Fold the batting in fourths to find the center and mark. With the batting on a flat surface, center the 3½" x 7" novelty print piece on top. Pin in place; then stitch ⅛" from the raw edges.

7. Place a piece of chenille face up alongside the center panel on each long edge. Pin in place. Stitch ⅛" from the raw edges. Center trim #1 over the butted raw edges of the center panel and the chenille. Edgestitch in place.

8. With right sides together and using a ¼"-wide seam allowance, stitch a border strip to the top and bottom edges of the pillow top. Flip the sashing onto the batting. Press and pin in place. Center trim #2 over the seam line and stitch in place.

9. Attach the gathering foot to your sewing machine and set the machine for the longest stitch length and the tightest tension. (If you do not have a gathering foot, try your machine without one. Play with the tension and stitch-length settings to make the fabric gather. If this doesn't work, see the "Designer Tip" below.) Test the stitch on a 12"- to 15"-long strip of scrap fabric. The stitching should reduce the length of the strip by ⅓. If these settings create gathers that are too tight, reduce the tension and then the stitch length until the desired results are achieved.

10. Gather both long edges of each of the 4" x 12" strips so they match the length of the pillow.

> **DESIGNER TIP**
> If you do not have a gathering foot, machine baste ¼" and ⅜" from each long raw edge of each 4" x 22" puffing strip. Draw up the gathers to fit the short edge of the pillow top. Draw up the remaining edge to match. After attaching the puffing strip to the batting and adding the trim, remove any basting stitches that show.

11. With right sides up, pin a puffing strip to each short edge of the pillow, overlapping it ⅛". Stitch to the batting. Center trim #3 over the raw edges and stitch in place (refer to the photo).

12. Square and trim the pillow top so the batting is even with the patchwork. Stitch the puffing strip in place ⅛" from outer raw edges.

13. Embellish the center panel with buttons (refer to the photo).

Finishing

1. Measure the completed pillow top and cut a piece of backing fabric to match (approximately 13¾" x 19¾"). Place the completed pillow top face down on the right side of the backing; pin.

2. Stitch ¼" from the raw edges, leaving an opening large enough for your hand to fit through. Backstitch at the beginning and end of the stitching. Turn right side out through the opening.

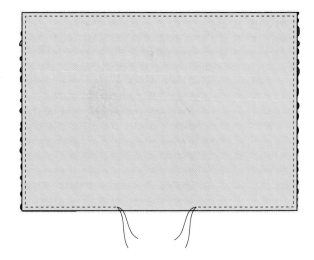

3. Stuff with polyester fiberfill to the desired fullness.

4. Close the opening with tiny hand slipstitches.

This pillow is sure to start a "colorful" conversation in a child's room! Juvenile prints make great center panels—and kids will love the soft texture of the chenille. Why not let them choose the fabric and buttons and help with the straight stitching, too? Who knows? You could have a budding quilt artist on your hands!

Twist and Tuck

Twist and Tuck, 21" x 21", Judy Murrah, December 1999, Victoria, Texas.

Three-dimensional "biscuits" take center stage in this textured design. Machine pintucks add even more texture to this colorful pillow.

Materials

➤ 4 squares muslin, each 3" x 3", for flat biscuit center panel

➤ 4 squares printed fabric (4 different prints), each 4" x 4", for flat biscuit center panel

➤ 2 strips stripe or print, each 3" x 5½", for flat biscuit center panel

➤ 1 strip solid or tone-on-tone print fabric, 9" x 22", for pintucked strips

➤ 1 strip coordinating print, 3½" x 28", for top and bottom borders

➤ 1 strip coordinating print, 2" x 33", for side borders

➤ 2 strips coordinating solid, each 3" x 40", for pillow flange

➤ 1 square, 23" x 23", of firm batting such as Warm & Natural needled cotton batting or Fairfield Cotton for foundation

➤ Perle cotton thread, size 8, for embellishment

- ➤ Large-eyed, hand embroidery needle for sewing with perle cotton thread
- ➤ Pintucking foot for sewing machine
- ➤ Twin needle for sewing machine
- ➤ ⅓ yd. trim #1 for embellishment
- ➤ ⅔ yd. trim #2 for embellishment
- ➤ ¾ yd. trim #3 for embellishment
- ➤ 1 yd. trim #4 for embellishment
- ➤ ½ yd. 45"-wide or 54"-wide print fabric for pillow backing
- ➤ 16" x 16" pillow form
- ➤ 3 flat, ⅝"-diameter buttons for pillow closure

Assembly

1. Mark the center of each side of each muslin square.

2. With the right side up, pin 2 corners of a 4" print biscuit square to the upper edge of a 3" muslin square at the corners. Because the print square is larger, there will be excess fabric in the center.

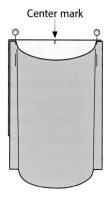

Center mark

3. Working from left to right and with raw edges even, pin the edge of the biscuit square to the muslin at the center mark. Then fold the remainder of the biscuit square back on itself to form a pleat. Pin in place. Continue around the square clockwise, working in the same fashion until all 4 edges are pleated and pinned. Stitch ⅛" from the raw edges. Make the remaining biscuits in the same manner.

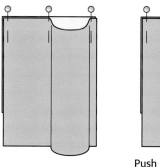

Push excess toward left and make pleat.

4. Arrange the excess fabric to make a folded box in the center of the square and press.

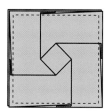

5. With right sides together, stitch the biscuits together in pairs. Press the seams in opposite directions. Stitch the pairs together to make a Four Patch block. Press the seam in one direction.

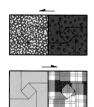

6. Fold the 23" square of batting in half and then in half again and mark the center. Working on a flat surface, center the biscuit panel on the batting and pin in place. Using 2 strands of perle cotton, stitch a large X in the center of the biscuit unit to anchor it to the batting, making each stitch ¾" long.

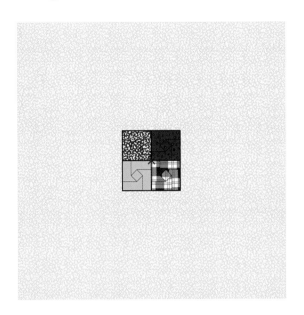

7. To tack the center of each biscuit to the batting, thread a single strand of perle cotton in the needle but do not knot the end. Take a stitch from the right side through to the back and then back to the right side, taking a ¼" bite of fabric. Tie the thread in a double knot on the right side of the biscuit center. Clip threads, leaving ½"-long tails.

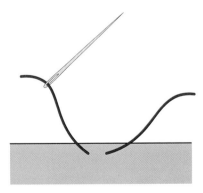

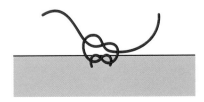

8. With right sides together, stitch the 3" x 5½" fabric strips to the top and bottom edges of the biscuits, stitching ¼" from the raw edges. Press the strips toward the batting and pin in place ("stitch and flip"; see page 23).

9. Topstitch trim #1 along the seam lines.

10. Replace your regular presser foot with a pintucking foot.

Pintucking foot

11. Insert a twin needle in your machine and thread machine with 2 spools of matching or contrasting color thread, placing 1 thread to the left and 1 thread to the right of the tension disc. Take care not to cross them as you complete the threading.

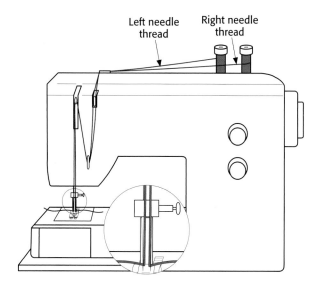

Left needle thread   Right needle thread

12. Beginning an inch from the raw edge, do rows of pintucking parallel to the short end of the pin-tucking fabric strip. After stitching the first row, leave the thread attached, rotate the fabric, and stitch the next row in the opposite direction, spacing it a presser foot's width from the first row. Continue stitching in this manner until you have an 11"-long pintucked strip. Trim away excess untucked fabric, and then cut the tucked strip into 2 pieces, each 4½" x 11".

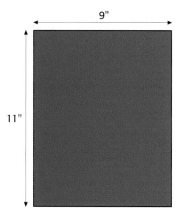

9"

11"

13. Sew a tucked strip to opposite long edges of the biscuit unit, using the stitch-and-flip method described earlier. Position and topstitch trim #2 in place over the seam lines.

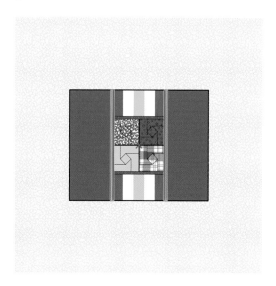

14. Cut the 3½" x 28" strip in half crosswise and stitch and flip the strips to opposite ends of the biscuit/pintucked unit. Position and topstitch trim #3 in place over the seam lines.

15. Repeat step 6, using the 2" x 33" fabric strip and sew to the remaining edges of the biscuit/pintucked unit. Position and topstitch trim #4 in place over the seam lines. The patchwork pillow top is now complete and should measure 16½" square. If it's slightly smaller, don't worry. Pillow covers look best when they are a little snug.

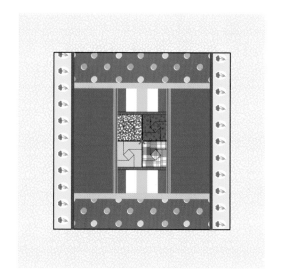

Finishing

1. Cut two 16½"-long strips from 1 of the flange strips. Stitch and flip to opposite edges of the pillow top. From the remaining flange strip, cut two 21½"-long strips. Stitch and flip to the remaining edges of the pillow top. The piece should now measure 21½" square. Trim excess batting even with the pillow top, squaring up the pillow top if necessary. Stitch ⅛" from the raw edges to secure pillow top to batting edge.

2. From the pillow backing fabric, cut 2 pieces, each 13" x 21½". On each piece, turn under and press ½" on one long edge, and then turn again and edgestitch close to the inner edge of the hem. Press. Make 3 vertical buttonholes in one of the pieces, spacing them as shown.

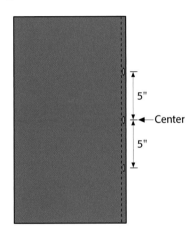

5"

Center

5"

Space buttonholes as shown.

3. With right sides together and raw edges even, pin the backing piece with the buttonholes to the pillow top.

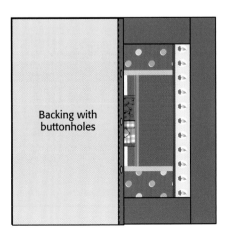

Backing with buttonholes

4. Place the remaining backing piece face down on top and pin in place. Stitch ¼" from all raw edges.

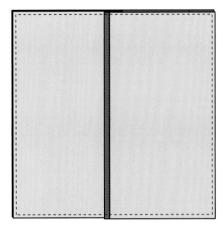

5. Turn the top right side out. Press, making sure that all 4 corners are neatly turned and pressed. Sew buttons in position on the backing underneath the buttonholes.

6. Stitch in the ditch at the seam of the flange seam to secure the flange to the backing, being careful to keep the backing flat and smooth while you stitch.

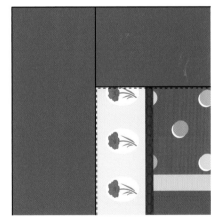

Stitch in the ditch through all layers.

7. Insert pillow form and button up!

Isn't it fun?

Wedges and Ruffles

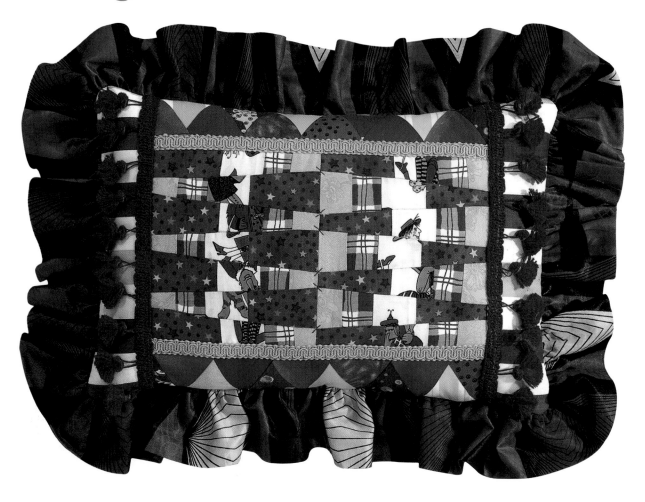

Wedges and Ruffles, 17" x 23", Judy Murrah, December 1999, Victoria, Texas.

Strong colors and simple patchwork shapes make this pillow a real eye catcher. For a touch of whimsy, use a conversational print for one of the four patchwork fabrics. Tassled trim makes the pillow even more playful.

Materials

- 1 strip fabric #1, 3" x 22", for wedge center
- 1 strip fabric #2, 1½" x 22", for wedge center
- 1 strip fabric #3, 2" x 22", for wedge center
- 1 strip fabric #4, 1½" x 22", for wedge center
- Scraps in 3 colors for triangles in top and bottom borders
- 2 strips, each 3" x 12", for side borders
- ½ yd. print for ruffle
- ½ yd. print or solid for backing

- 12½" x 18½" firm batting such as Warm & Natural needled cotton batting or Fairfield Cotton batting for foundation
- ⅔ yd. braid #1 (½" wide) for embellishment
- ⅔ yd. braid #2 (with tassels) for embellishment
- Perle cotton or embroidery floss for embellishment
- Polyester fiberfill for stuffing pillow
- Gathering foot for sewing machine (optional)

NOTE: *All seams are ¼" wide.*

Use the patterns on page 94 to make Templates A and B.

Assembly

1. Arrange the strips of fabrics #1–4 as desired and sew together. The fabrics in the center of the strip-pieced unit will be the most dominant in the finished piece. Press the seams in the direction indicated by the arrows.

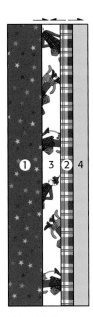

Use this layout, or arrange in any other desired order.

2. Cut wedges using Template A. Position the template with the wide end at the top and cut the first wedge. Turn the template so the narrow end is up to cut the next wedge. Continue alternating the template direction and cutting until you have 14 wedges.

Template A

Cut 14 wedges.

3. Divide the wedges into 2 stacks of matching wedges.

Stack 1   Stack 2

4. Working with one stack of wedges at a time, sew them together, wide end to narrow, to make a piece of patchwork. Press the seams in the direction indicated by the arrows. There will be a little "twist" in each seam.

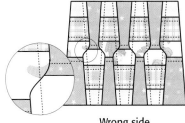

Wrong side

5. Use a rotary cutter, ruler, and mat to square up each piece. They should be the same size and shape.

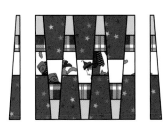

6. Sew the 2 pieces of patchwork together matching the seams. It is helpful to turn 1 seam in each pair in the opposite direction so the seams can snug into each other for a perfect match. When the stitching is completed, there will be a little "twist" in the seam. Press open the joining seam.

7. Center the wedge panel on the batting. Pin in place. Stitch ⅛" from the long edges.

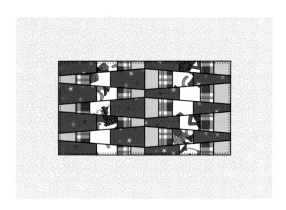

8. By hand, make ¼"-long stab stitches out from each center seam intersection. Use a strand of perle cotton or 2 strands of embroidery floss.

9. Using Template B and scraps of fabric, cut a total of 24 triangles for the top and bottom borders (12 for each border). Cut 12 of Color #1 and 6 each of colors #2 and #3.

10. Following the illustration, arrange the triangles in 2 rows of 12 triangles each.

11. With right sides facing, chain piece the triangles together in pairs. Cut apart at thread chains and press the seam in each pair toward the darker fabric. Trim away the seam allowance "ear" that extends beyond the seam.

Press toward darker fabric.

Trim ears.

12. Stitch each triangle pair to its neighboring pair as shown. Press toward the darker fabric and trim the "ear."

Points extend beyond straight edges.

Trim ear.

13. Continue sewing the pairs together in the same manner until you have 2 strips of 12 triangles each. Trim the ends perpendicular to the long edges.

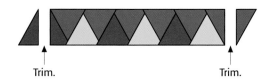

Trim.   Trim.

14. Pin triangle strips to the batting on opposite side of the center wedge panel, leaving ¼" of space between the raw edges. Stitch ⅛" from each long edge of each triangle strip.

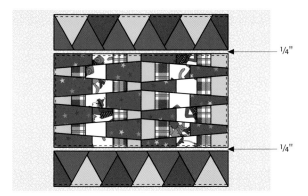

15. Center braid #1 over the raw edges and edgestitch in place.

16. Stitch and flip a 3" x 12" side border to each short end of the pillow top. Press and pin to the batting. Center and stitch tasseled trim (braid #2) over the seam lines.

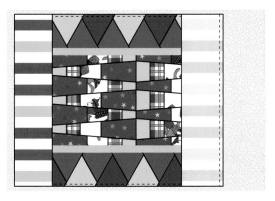

Stitch and flip borders in place.

Finishing

1. Trim and square up the patchwork and batting. The finished piece should measure approximately 12" x 18". Stitch ⅛" from the outer raw edges. Cut a piece of pillow backing fabric to match the size and shape of the pillow top.

2. From the ruffle fabric, cut 3 strips, each 5" wide, cutting across the fabric width. Sew the short ends of the strips together to make a circle of fabric and press the seams open.

Sew strips together in a circle.

3. Fold the ruffle strip in half lengthwise with the wrong sides together and press.

4. Gather the ruffle to half its original length. Use the gathering foot on your machine (see step 9 on page 84 or follow the directions in the "Designer Tip" on page 84).

5. Pin the ruffle to the right side of the pillow top with raw edges even. Adjust the gathers so there are a few more gathers at the corners. Stitch in place along the line of gathering stitches. You will need to round the corners as shown.

More fullness at corners

> **DESIGNER TIP**
> If the ruffle is too large, use the point of a pin to lift and pull up on the gathering stitches at random intervals to draw it in to fit. If it is a little too small, you can "pop" a few stitches here and there to release a little of the gathering.

6. Sandwiching the ruffle between the pillow top and the pillow backing, pin the layers together with raw edges even. Make sure the ruffle is inside the layers, out of the way of the stitching. I pin it to the pillow top to make sure it stays out of the way. Stitch through all thicknesses, leaving an opening the size of your hand for turning and stuffing.

7. Turn the pillow right side out and stuff with polyester fiberfill. Stitch the opening closed with small hand slipstitches.

Who says pillows can't have lots of pizzazz? This one sure does!

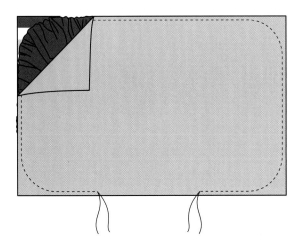

Wedges and Ruffles
Patterns

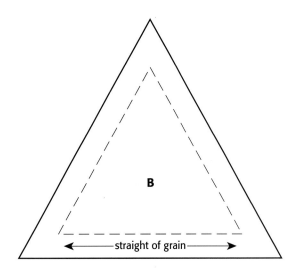

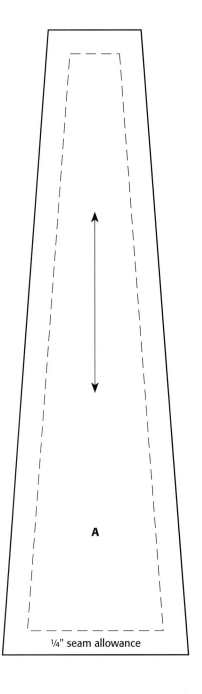

About the Author

In the Studio with Judy Murrah is Judy Murrah's sixth book to be published by Martingale & Company. Other books include *Jacket Jazz, Jacket Jazz Encore, More Jazz, Dress Daze,* and *Jazz It Up.* Her pattern line, Judy Murrah Originals, includes designs for six different garments. She has also worn the hat of fabric designer for Clothworks, basing her fabric designs for "Jacket Jazz in Another Key" on her ever popular, embellished patchwork garment designs. For information on Judy's classes and correspondence courses, write to her at 109 Pasadena Drive, Victoria, Texas 77904. Include a self-addressed stamped envelope.

Judy has been Director of Education for Quilts, Inc., for over fifteen years and is the co-founder of the Quilt Guild of Greater Victoria. She lives with her husband, Tom, in Victoria, Texas, and has three grown children, a daughter-in-law, a son-in-law, and two grandchildren.